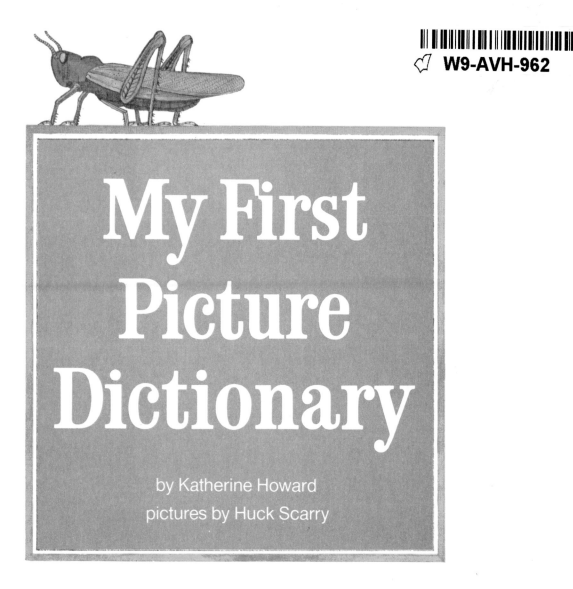

My First Picture Dictionary

by Katherine Howard

pictures by Huck Scarry

Random House 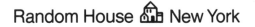 New York

29 30

A Random House PICTUREBACK®

A B C D E F G H I J K L M N O P Q R S T U V W X Y Z

A a

Aardvark–An African animal that eats ants and termites.

Acorn–The nut of an oak tree.

OAK TREE
CAP
NUT
OAK LEAF

Acrobat–A person trained to do difficult stunts.

Airplane–A vehicle with wings that travels through the air.

WRIGHT BROTHERS' PLANE

SPIRIT OF ST. LOUIS

X-15 JET

JUMBO JET AIRLINER

SUPERSONIC TRANSPORT

Alarm clock–A clock that can be set to ring at certain times.

BELL

Alligator–A large reptile with a long head and tail, and very sharp teeth.

EGG

Ambulance–A special car that carries sick or hurt people to and from the hospital.

STRETCHER

Animal–Any living thing that is not a plant and can move about. Tiny ants, big elephants, and people, too, are animals.

STARFISH
DOG
SEAL

Ant–A small insect that lives underground with many other ants in a colony.

ANT HILL

ANTENNAE

Apple–A green, yellow, or red fruit that grows on trees.

APPLE TREE

Astronaut–A person trained to be a pilot or crew member of a spaceship.

HELMET

BACKPACK

GLOVE

BOOT

Antlers–The bony horns that grow on the head of male deer, elks, and moose.

DEER

MOOSE

Aquarium–A bowl or tank in which people keep water animals or plants.

AIR PUMP

Automobile–A kind of vehicle that has its own engine. A car.

WORM

SEA GULL

LADYBUG

FISH

HUMAN BEING

SNAIL

GIRAFFE

HORSE

TAILLIGHT

TRUNK

RADIO ANTENNA

ROOF

DOOR

HOOD

TIRE

BUMPER

HEADLIGHT

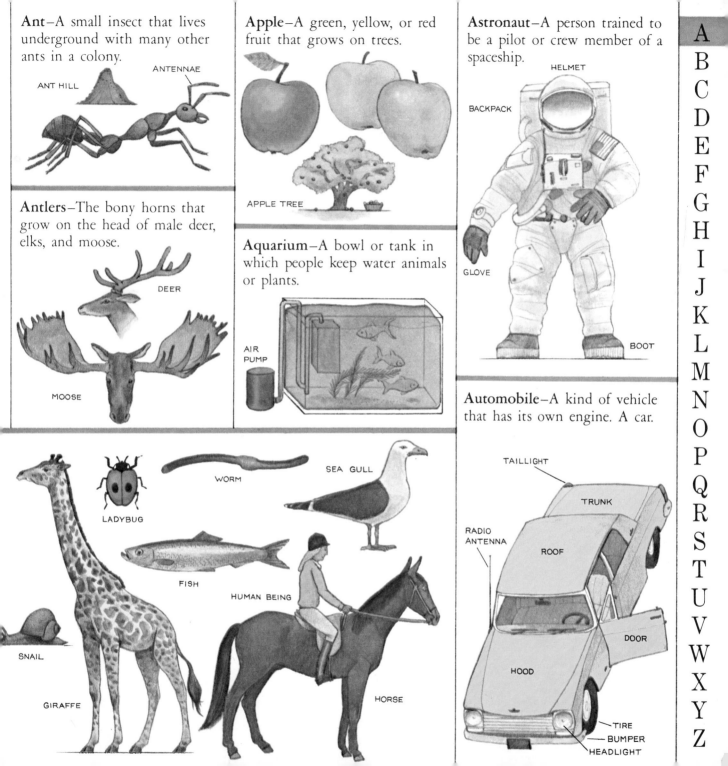

B b

Ball–A round, or almost round, object used to play games.

SOCCER BALL

BASEBALL

FOOTBALL

BASKETBALL

Banana–A yellow fruit that grows on tall treelike plants in warm countries.

Bandage—A clean piece of cloth used to cover a cut or wound. Sometimes it is attached to a strip of tape.

Barn–A large farm building where animals and their food are kept.

LOFT

SILO

HAY

Basket–A container made of woven strips of wood, straw, or other material.

Bed–A piece of furniture used to sleep on.

Beetle–An insect with two hard outer wings.

RHINOCEROS BEETLE

LADYBUG

STAG BEETLE

Beach–The land along the edge of an ocean, lake, or other body of water.

LIFEGUARD

LIGHTHOUSE

BUOY

WAVES

SHORE

DRIFTWOOD

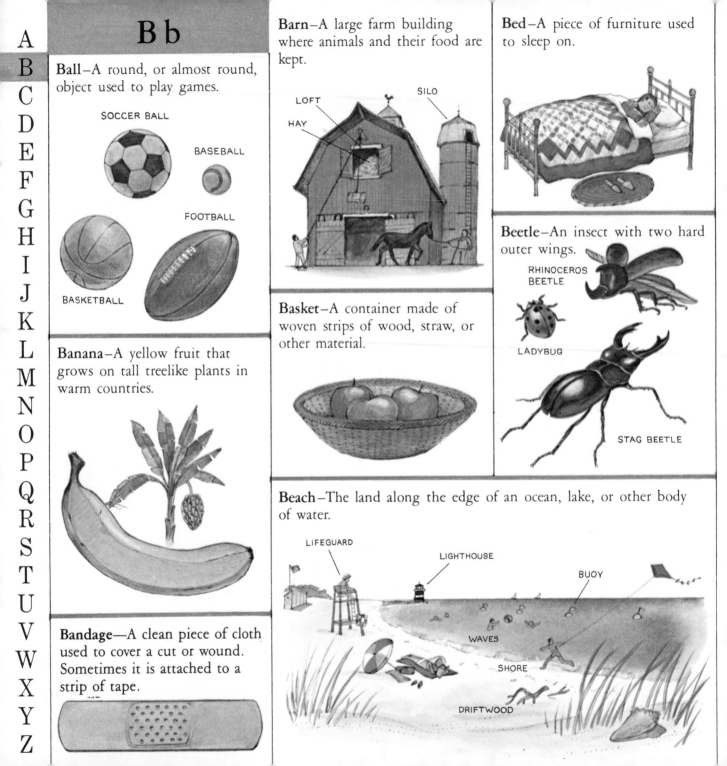

Bicycle–A light vehicle with two wheels that is driven by foot pedals.

HANDLEBARS
SEAT
HAND BRAKES
PEDAL
WHEELS

Bird–An animal with feathers, two wings, and two legs. Most birds can fly.

ROBIN
EYE
WING
BEAK
EGG
BREAST
TAIL
LEGS
CLAWS
OSTRICH
PENGUIN
DUCK

Boat–A vehicle for traveling on water. Oars, paddles, sails, and engines are all used to move boats.

ROWBOAT
STERN
OAR
MOTORBOAT
OUTBOARD MOTOR
STARBOARD SIDE
OARLOCK
PORT SIDE
BOW
KAYAK
INFLATABLE BOAT

Body–All the parts of a person or animal.

HEAD
EYEBROW
HAIR
EAR
EYE
NOSE
MOUTH
NECK
CHIN
SHOULDER
CHEST
ARM
WRIST
ELBOW
STOMACH
HAND
FINGERS
LEG
THIGH
KNEE
SHIN
CALF
ANKLE
FOOT
TOES

Book–Sheets of printed paper fastened between two covers.

PAGE
COVER
SPINE

Bread–A food made mostly with flour.

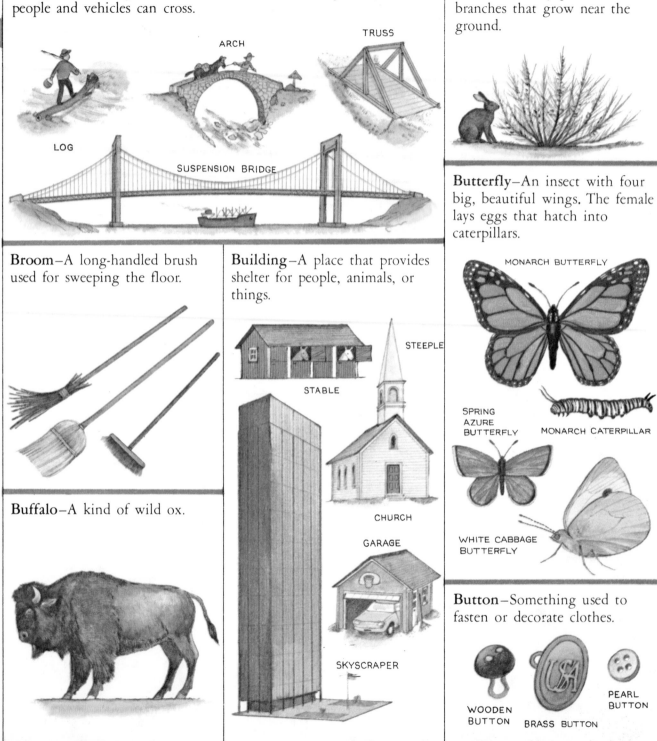

A B C D E F G H I J K L M N O P Q R S T U V W X Y Z

Bridge–Something built across water, roads, or deep valleys so people and vehicles can cross.

LOG

ARCH

TRUSS

SUSPENSION BRIDGE

Broom–A long-handled brush used for sweeping the floor.

Buffalo–A kind of wild ox.

Building–A place that provides shelter for people, animals, or things.

STABLE

STEEPLE

CHURCH

GARAGE

SKYSCRAPER

Bush–A woody plant with branches that grow near the ground.

Butterfly–An insect with four big, beautiful wings. The female lays eggs that hatch into caterpillars.

MONARCH BUTTERFLY

SPRING AZURE BUTTERFLY

MONARCH CATERPILLAR

WHITE CABBAGE BUTTERFLY

Button–Something used to fasten or decorate clothes.

WOODEN BUTTON

BRASS BUTTON

PEARL BUTTON

C c

Cabin–A small house, usually made of wood.

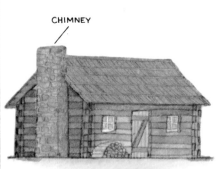

CHIMNEY

Cactus–A plant that has spines and thick stems that store water.

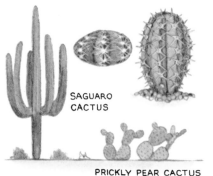

SAGUARO CACTUS

PRICKLY PEAR CACTUS

Camel–A big animal with one or two humps on its back.

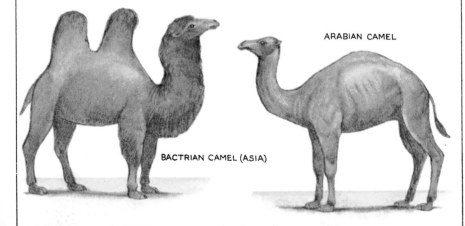

BACTRIAN CAMEL (ASIA)

ARABIAN CAMEL

Camera–A box with moving parts inside that is used to take photographs or movies.

LENS

STUDIO CAMERA

TELEVISION CAMERA

Canoe–A long, light boat moved with paddles.

PADDLE

Car–A motor vehicle with four wheels. An automobile.

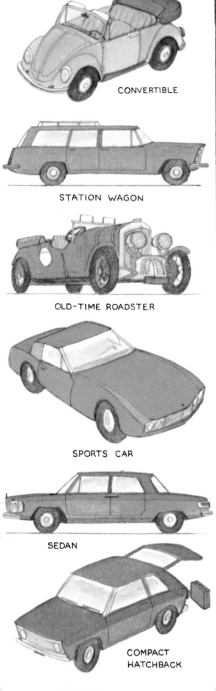

CONVERTIBLE

STATION WAGON

OLD-TIME ROADSTER

SPORTS CAR

SEDAN

COMPACT HATCHBACK

A
B
C
D
E
F
G
H
I
J
K
L
M
N
O
P
Q
R
S
T
U
V
W
X
Y
Z

A B C D E F G H I J K L M N O P Q R S T U V W X Y Z

Castle–A large building with towers and thick walls, often surrounded by a moat. Castles were built to keep out enemies.

LOOKOUT TOWER

TOWER

COURTYARD

DRAWBRIDGE

MOAT

Cat–A small furry animal, often kept as a pet.

Chain–A row of rings or links connected to each other.

Clothes–Things people wear to cover their bodies.

SHIRT

HAT

COAT

SWEATER

UNDERWEAR

PANTS

SOCKS

SHOES

Clown–Someone who dresses in funny clothes and performs funny stunts in the circus.

Cobweb–A network of fine, sticky threads spun by spiders to catch insects.

Color–Red, yellow, and blue are the three basic colors. They can be mixed to make many other colors.

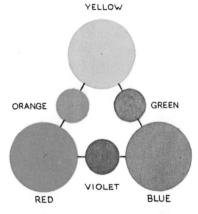

YELLOW

ORANGE

GREEN

RED

VIOLET

BLUE

Cowboy–A person who works on a cattle ranch.

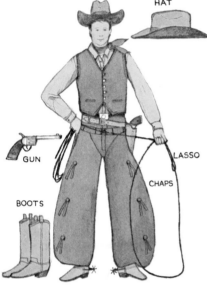

HAT

GUN

LASSO

CHAPS

BOOTS

Crab–A sea animal with a hard shell, eight legs, and two strong front claws.

Cucumber–A green vegetable that grows on low vines.

D d

Dandelion–A wild plant. A weed.

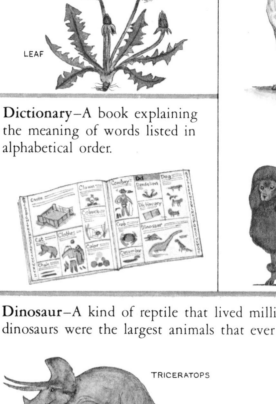

FLOWER

SEEDS

LEAF

Dictionary–A book explaining the meaning of words listed in alphabetical order.

Dinosaur–A kind of reptile that lived millions of years ago. Some dinosaurs were the largest animals that ever lived on land.

TRICERATOPS

PALAEOSCINUS

TYRANNOSAURUS

BRONTOSAURUS

Dog–A four-legged animal, often kept as a pet. There are many different kinds of dogs.

DACHSHUND

POINTER

PUG

POODLE

A B C D E F G H I J K L M N O P Q R S T U V W X Y Z

Doll–A toy made to look like a person.

SPOOL DOLL

PLASTIC DOLL

Dolphin–A playful, long-nosed sea animal that is related to the whale.

Duck–A bird with a flat beak and webbed feet for swimming.

WILD DUCK

DOMESTIC DUCK

E e

Eagle–A large bird with powerful claws and wings.

GOLDEN EAGLE

Elephant–The largest and strongest land animal.

Engine–A machine that supplies power to make something work.

Escalator–A moving staircase.

Eskimo–One of a people that live in cold, arctic lands.

PARKA

MITTEN

KAYAK

IGLOO

F f

Fan–A machine or object used to move the air.

HAND FAN

ELECTRIC FAN

Farm–An area of land, including buildings, where crops and animals are raised for food.

FIELD

FARMHOUSE

BARN

PIGPEN

FARMER

SILO

MANURE

ORCHARD

HENS

Fish–An animal that lives in the water. Fish have fins and breathe through gills.

FINS

EYE

TAIL

MOUTH

GILL

SCALES

MINNOWS

BARRACUDA

Feather–One of the light, soft growths that cover a bird's skin.

DOWN

Ferry–A boat that takes people, cars, and other things back and forth across a body of water.

Fireman–A person trained to put out fires.

LADDER

HELMET

PIKE

SLICKER

AX

BOOTS

Flag–A piece of cloth with a design in color that stands for a country or an organization.

UNITED STATES

CANADA

RED CROSS

UNITED NATIONS

PENNANT

A
B
C
D
E
F
G
H
I
J
K
L
M
N
O
P
Q
R
S
T
U
V
W
X
Y
Z

A
B
C
D
E
F
G
H
I
J
K
L
M
N
O
P
Q
R
S
T
U
V
W
X
Y
Z

Flower–The part of a plant that has colorful petals.

POPPY

STIGMA

STAMEN

DAISY

SEPAL

PETAL

STEM

DAFFODIL

TULIP

ROSE

Frog–A small animal with webbed feet and strong hind legs for jumping.

Food–Anything that is eaten by people or animals to help them grow.

CHEESE

EGG

TOMATO

MILK

MEAT

BREAD

Fork–A tool used for eating food.

KNIFE

SPOON

Fossil–Any trace or the remains of an animal or plant that lived long ago.

Fox–A wild animal with a bushy tail, pointed ears, and a doglike body.

Fruit–The part of a plant in which you find the seeds. Many fruits are good to eat.

CHERRY

ELM SEED

MAPLE SEEDS

SEED

APPLE

STRAWBERRY

DANDELION SEED

Furniture–The movable things in a house or building, such as chairs, tables, beds, or sofas.

CHAIR DESK

SOFA

BENCH

TABLE

Grape–A small, sweet fruit that grows in bunches on a vine.

VINE

BUNCH OF GRAPES

G g

Garage–A building in which cars and trucks are parked or repaired.

GASOLINE PUMP

Gerbil–A small, furry animal that jumps like a kangaroo. Gerbils make good pets.

Glove–A piece of clothing with five fingers that fits over the hand.

Goat–A hoofed animal that has two short horns.

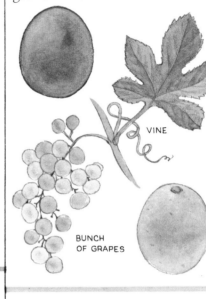

HOOF

Grasshopper–An insect with strong hind legs used for hopping.

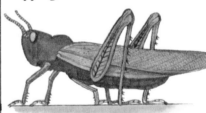

Guitar–A musical instrument that has six or more strings.

TUNING PEGS

A
B
C
D
E
F
G
H
I
J
K
L
M
N
O
P
Q
R
S
T
U
V
W
X
Y
Z

H h

Hammer–A hand tool used for pounding nails.

HANDLE · HEAD

Handbag–A bag that is light enough to carry by hand.

Hat–A covering for the head.

CROWN · CAP · BRIM · FELT HAT · BERET

Helicopter–An aircraft that has large rotor blades. It can take off, land, or fly straight up and down.

Helmet–A hard hat worn to protect the head.

KNIGHT'S HELMET · SOLDIER'S HELMET · FOOTBALL HELMET · MOTORCYCLE HELMET

Hippopotamus–A huge African animal that spends a lot of time in the water.

Harbor–A sheltered place where ships dock for loading and unloading or for repairs.

LIGHTHOUSE · HARBOR MASTER · CHANNEL · JETTY · CRANE · MOORINGS · DOCK · RAMP · QUAY

Horse–A large hoofed animal used for riding or pulling loads.

MANE · HOOF

A B C D E F G H I J K L M N O P Q R S T U V W X Y Z

House–A building that is used for living in.

APARTMENT HOUSE

COLONIAL

DOGHOUSE

THATCH HUT

COTTAGE

Hummingbird–A tiny bird that moves its wings so fast they make a humming sound.

I i

Ice–Water that has been frozen solid.

Iceberg–A large piece of ice that floats in the ocean.

Ice cream–A sweet, frozen food made from cream.

CONE

POPSICLE

Ice skates–Boots with metal blades for skating on ice.

HOCKEY SKATES

Insect–A very small animal with six legs. Most insects have wings. There are more than 800,000 kinds of insects.

LADYBUG

ANT

HONEYBEE

FLEA

DRAGONFLY

Iron–A tool that, when heated, presses wrinkles out of clothes.

IRONING BOARD

A B C D E F G H I J K L M N O P Q R S T U V W X Y Z

J j

Jacket–A short coat.

WINDBREAKER

BLAZER

Jack-o'-lantern–A hollow pumpkin with a face carved out of one side.

Jar–A container with a wide opening.

Jeep–A powerful car that can drive over rough roads or fields.

SPARE TIRE

GAS TANK

WINDSHIELD

BUMPER

Jellyfish–A sea animal with a jellylike body and long tentacles.

Jug–A container that has a handle and a small opening.

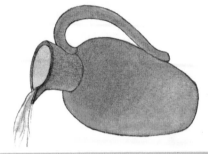

Jungle–A thick tangle of vines, bushes, and trees growing in a hot, wet place.

Jet–An airplane driven by a special, powerful engine.

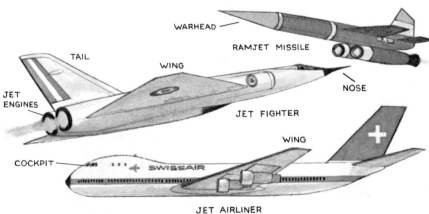

WARHEAD

RAMJET MISSILE

TAIL

WING

NOSE

JET ENGINES

JET FIGHTER

WING

COCKPIT

SWISSAIR

JET AIRLINER

K k

Kangaroo
Kangaroo–A large Australian animal. The female carries her young in a pouch.

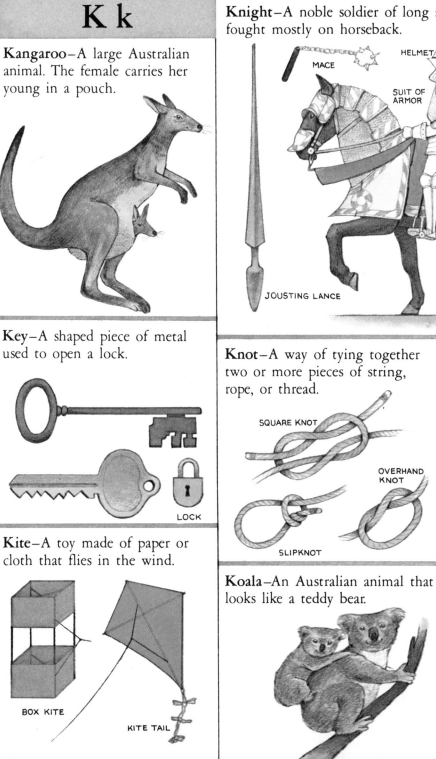

Key–A shaped piece of metal used to open a lock.

LOCK

Kite–A toy made of paper or cloth that flies in the wind.

BOX KITE

KITE TAIL

Knight–A noble soldier of long ago. Knights wore armor and fought mostly on horseback.

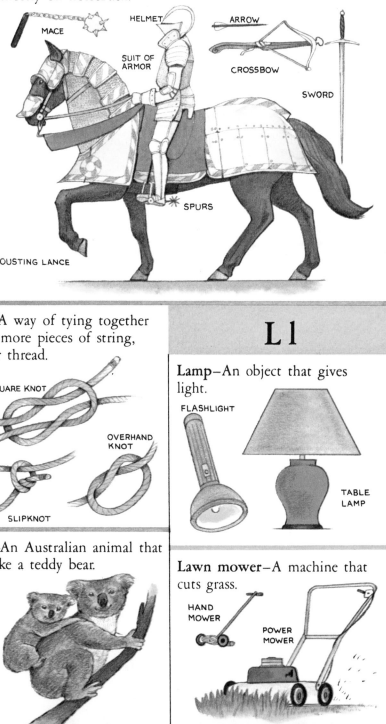

MACE
HELMET
ARROW
SUIT OF ARMOR
CROSSBOW
SWORD
SPURS
JOUSTING LANCE

Knot–A way of tying together two or more pieces of string, rope, or thread.

SQUARE KNOT
OVERHAND KNOT
SLIPKNOT

Koala–An Australian animal that looks like a teddy bear.

L l

Lamp–An object that gives light.

FLASHLIGHT
TABLE LAMP

Lawn mower–A machine that cuts grass.

HAND MOWER
POWER MOWER

A
B
C
D
E
F
G
H
I
J
K
L
M
N
O
P
Q
R
S
T
U
V
W
X
Y
Z

Leaf–The flat, green part of a plant that grows on the stem.

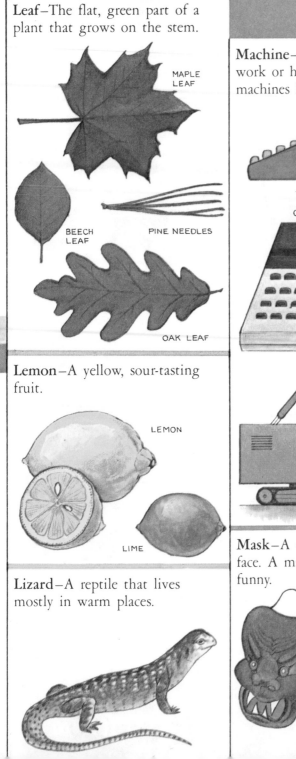

MAPLE LEAF

BEECH LEAF

PINE NEEDLES

OAK LEAF

Lemon–A yellow, sour-tasting fruit.

LEMON

LIME

Lizard–A reptile that lives mostly in warm places.

M m

Machine–Something that does work or helps with a job. Often machines have moving parts.

TYPEWRITER

CALCULATOR

1000.

CRANE

Mask–A cover to hide a person's face. A mask can be scary or funny.

PAPER-BAG MASK

Mole–A small, furry animal that lives underground.

Money–Bills and coins used to pay people and buy things.

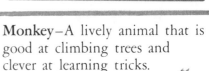

PENNY

NICKEL

DIME

QUARTER

DOLLAR BILL

THE UNITED STATES OF AMERICA

1978

Monkey–A lively animal that is good at climbing trees and clever at learning tricks.

LANGUR

BABOON

Moon–The earth's closest neighbor in space. The moon circles the earth every 29½ days.

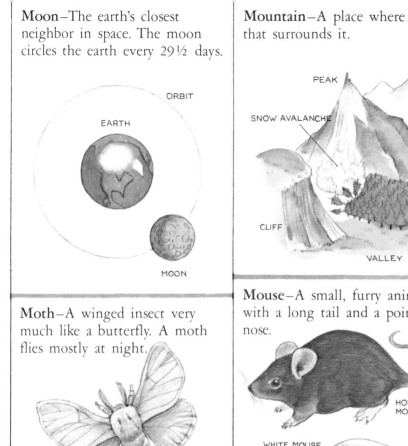

ORBIT

EARTH

MOON

Mountain–A place where the land rises far above the ground that surrounds it.

SUMMIT

PEAK

SNOW AVALANCHE

GLACIER

VOLCANO

FOOTHILL

CLIFF

LANDSLIDE

VALLEY

Moth–A winged insect very much like a butterfly. A moth flies mostly at night.

Mouse–A small, furry animal with a long tail and a pointed nose.

HOUSE MOUSE

WHITE MOUSE

Muffin–A sweet bread baked in the shape of a cup.

MUFFIN TIN

Mug–A heavy drinking cup with a handle.

Motorcycle–A two-wheeled vehicle, heavier than a bicycle and run by a motor.

CHOPPER

HANDLEBAR

GAS TANK

HEADLIGHT

MOTOR

WHEEL

Mushroom–A small, spongy, leafless plant, often shaped like an umbrella.

CAP

GILLS

STEM

A
B
C
D
E
F
G
H
I
J
K
L
M
N
O
P
Q
R
S
T
U
V
W
X
Y
Z

A B C D E F G H I J K L M N O P Q R S T U V W X Y Z

N n

Nail–A thin piece of metal with a sharp point, used to hold pieces of wood together.

TACK

Necktie–A piece of cloth worn around the neck, tied in a knot or bow.

BOW TIE

FOUR-IN-HAND

Nest–A place an animal prepares for laying its eggs or raising its babies.

BIRD'S NEST

MASON BEES' NEST

WOODPECKER'S NEST

Newt–A little animal that lives in or near the water.

Nut–A dry fruit or seed covered by a hard shell.

ALMOND

WALNUT

O o

Octopus–A sea animal with eight arms and a soft body.

TENTACLES

Onion–The strong-smelling bulb of a plant, eaten as a vegetable.

SPROUT

WHITE ONION

RINGS

SKIN

ROOTS

Ocean–A very large body of salt water. Oceans cover almost three-quarters of the earth.

BLUFF

OIL RIG

FISHING TRAWLER

SCUBA DIVER

SCHOOL OF FISH

FISHNET

OCTOPUS

SHIPWRECK

TREASURE

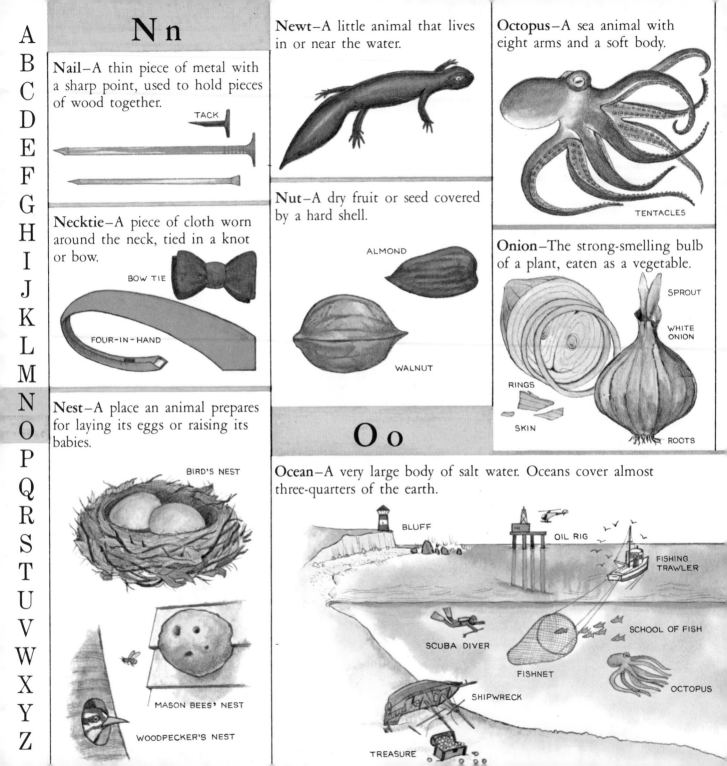

Orange–A round, reddish-yellow fruit with thick skin and sweet juice.

Orangutan–A large ape that lives in Asia. It has shaggy, reddish-brown fur.

Orchestra–A group of people who play different musical instruments together, under the direction of a conductor.

PIANO
TIMPANI
BASSOON
CLARINET
CELLO
FRENCH HORN
FLUTE
VIOLIN
MUSIC STAND
VIOLA
CONDUCTOR

Ostrich–The world's largest bird. The ostrich cannot fly.

Owl–A bird that sleeps during the day and hunts for food at night.

OCEAN LINER
CABIN CRUISER
SAILFISH
SHARKS
BATHYSCAPHE
WHALE

Overalls–Loose-fitting pants held up with shoulder straps.

Oyster–A small sea animal with a soft body inside a rough two-piece shell.

A B C D E F G H I J K L M N O P Q R S T U V W X Y Z

A
B
C
D
E
F
G
H
I
J
K
L
M
N
O
P
Q
R
S
T
U
V
W
X
Y
Z

P p

Parachute–An umbrella-shaped piece of cloth used to slow the fall from an airplane.

Parrot–A brightly colored bird with a strong bill. Some parrots can learn to repeat words.

Photograph–A picture taken by a camera.

PRINT

SLIDE

Piano–A large musical instrument with a keyboard.

KEYS

PEDALS

GRAND PIANO

Pillow–A cloth case filled with soft material on which you rest your head.

PILLOWCASE

Pineapple–A juicy fruit that grows in hot places.

Plant–A living thing that usually grows from roots. Most plants stay in one place and make their own food from air, sunlight, and water.

BLOSSOM

FRUIT

LEAVES

SEED

PEACH TREE

TRUNK

ROOTS

STRAWBERRY

CACTUS

WEED

GRASS

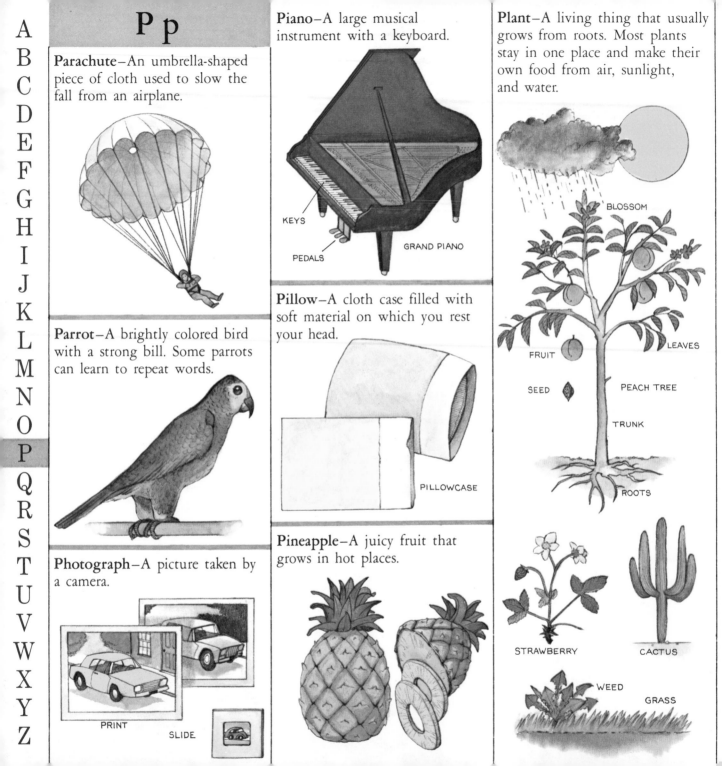

Pony–A kind of horse that is small even when it is full-grown.

Puppet–A doll that is moved by pulling strings or putting your hand inside it.

HAND PUPPET

MARIONETTE

Pyramid–An object with a square base and four sloping sides that come to a point.

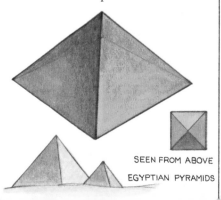

SEEN FROM ABOVE

EGYPTIAN PYRAMIDS

Q q

Quail–A plump ground bird that nests in tall grass.

Quarter–A coin that is worth twenty-five cents.

HEADS

TAILS

Quilt–A bedcover stuffed with soft material.

R r

Rabbit–A furry animal with long ears.

WILD RABBIT

DOMESTIC RABBIT

Reptile–One of a group of cold-blooded animals that crawl on their belly or on short legs. Most reptiles have rough, scaly skin, but turtles have tough shells.

CROCODILE

SNAKE

TURTLE

LIZARD

A B C D E F G H I J K L M N O P Q R S T U V W X Y Z

A
B
C
D
E
F
G
H
I
J
K
L
M
N
O
P
Q
R
S
T
U
V
W
X
Y
Z

Rhinoceros–A big, clumsy-looking animal with one or two horns on its snout.

Rice–A kind of grain that grows in shallow water. Rice is the most important food in Asia.

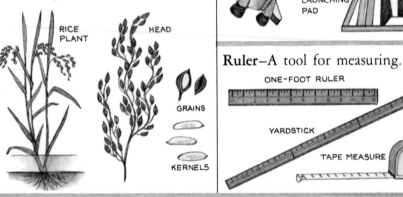

RICE PLANT

HEAD

GRAINS

KERNELS

River–A large stream of water that flows into another river, a lake, or an ocean.

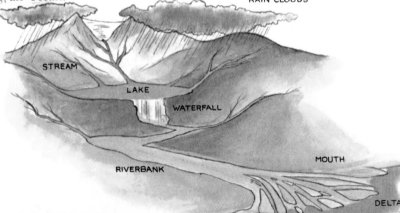

RAIN CLOUDS

STREAM

LAKE

WATERFALL

RIVERBANK

MOUTH

DELTA

Rocket–A machine that can be shot into space. Rockets have carried men to the moon.

GUIDED MISSILE

CAPSULE

THIRD STAGE

SECOND STAGE

SATURN V ROCKET

FIRST STAGE

V-2 ROCKET

LAUNCHING PAD

Ruler–A tool for measuring.

ONE-FOOT RULER

YARDSTICK

TAPE MEASURE

Sailboat–A boat that moves when the wind blows against its cloth sails.

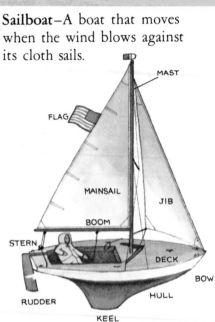

MAST

FLAG

MAINSAIL

JIB

BOOM

STERN

DECK

BOW

RUDDER

HULL

KEEL

Sandwich–Meat, jelly, cheese, or other food between slices of bread.

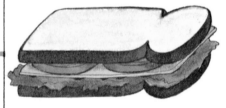

Scissors–A cutting tool with two sharp blades.

Sea shell–The hard covering that protects many kinds of sea animals.

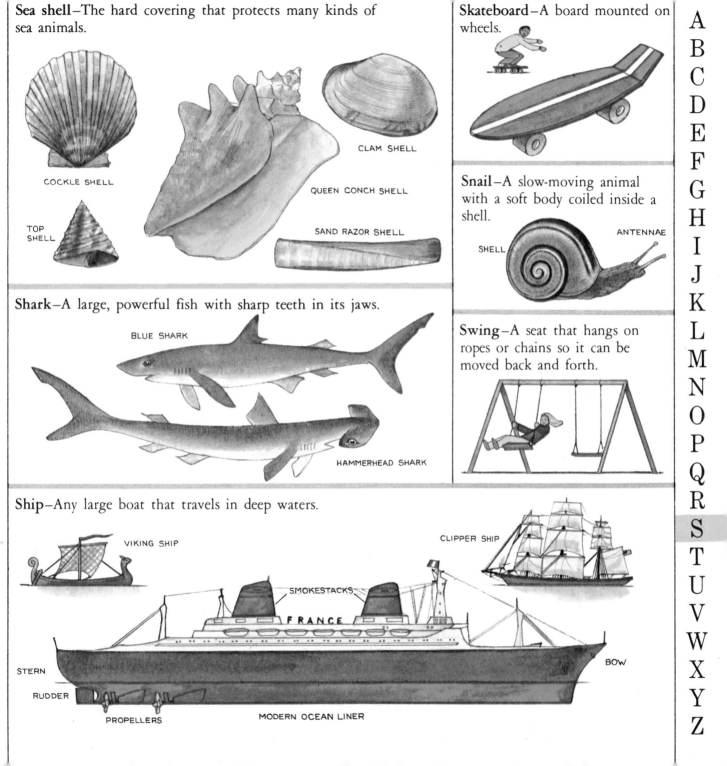

COCKLE SHELL

TOP SHELL

QUEEN CONCH SHELL

CLAM SHELL

SAND RAZOR SHELL

Shark–A large, powerful fish with sharp teeth in its jaws.

BLUE SHARK

HAMMERHEAD SHARK

Skateboard–A board mounted on wheels.

Snail–A slow-moving animal with a soft body coiled inside a shell.

SHELL

ANTENNAE

Swing–A seat that hangs on ropes or chains so it can be moved back and forth.

Ship–Any large boat that travels in deep waters.

VIKING SHIP

CLIPPER SHIP

SMOKESTACKS

FRANCE

STERN

RUDDER

PROPELLERS

MODERN OCEAN LINER

BOW

A B C D E F G H I J K L M N O P Q R S T U V W X Y Z

T t

Tadpole–A very young frog or toad. It lives under water.

EGG

TADPOLE

FROG

Television–A device that receives sound and pictures through the air.

COLOR TV

ANTENNA

SCREEN

PORTABLE TV

Tent–A shelter made of light material that can be easily carried.

CIRCUS TENT

CAMP TENT

GUIDELINE

PEG

DESERT NOMAD'S TENT

Thistle–A wild plant with prickly stalks and leaves. Usually it has purple flowers.

Tiger–A large, wild member of the cat family.

Toothbrush–A small brush used to clean the teeth.

BRISTLES

TUBE OF TOOTHPASTE

Tractor–A powerful vehicle used to pull machinery or heavy loads.

FARM TRACTOR

BULLDOZER

Tool–An instrument that people use to help them in doing work.

OPEN-END WRENCH

SCYTHE

SAW

PLIERS

PAINTBRUSHES

BLADE

COMPASS

PEN

Train–A string of railroad cars pulled along a track by an engine, or locomotive.

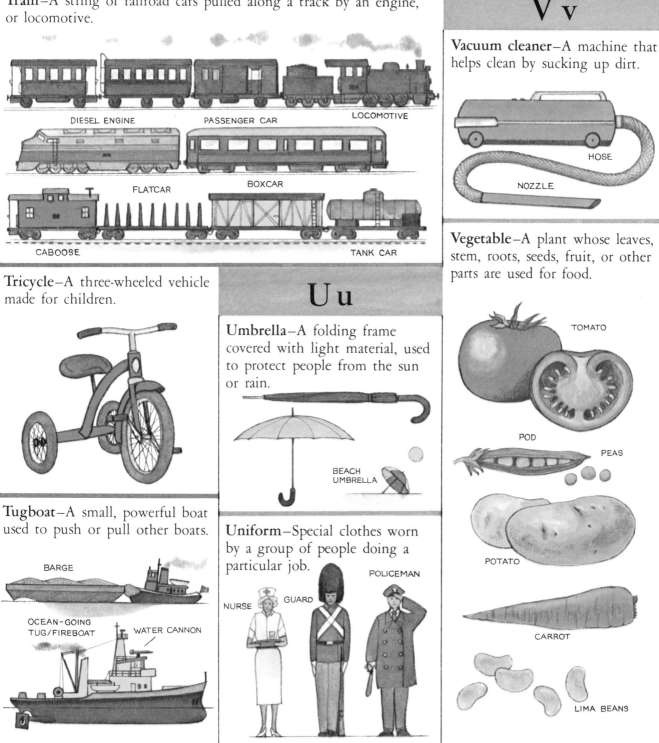

DIESEL ENGINE
PASSENGER CAR
LOCOMOTIVE
FLATCAR
BOXCAR
CABOOSE
TANK CAR

Tricycle–A three-wheeled vehicle made for children.

Tugboat–A small, powerful boat used to push or pull other boats.

BARGE
OCEAN-GOING TUG/FIREBOAT
WATER CANNON

U u

Umbrella–A folding frame covered with light material, used to protect people from the sun or rain.

BEACH UMBRELLA

Uniform–Special clothes worn by a group of people doing a particular job.

NURSE
GUARD
POLICEMAN

V v

Vacuum cleaner–A machine that helps clean by sucking up dirt.

HOSE
NOZZLE

Vegetable–A plant whose leaves, stem, roots, seeds, fruit, or other parts are used for food.

TOMATO
POD
PEAS
POTATO
CARROT
LIMA BEANS

A B C D E F G H I J K L M N O P Q R S T U V W X Y Z

Vehicle–Anything used to carry people or goods from one place to another.

SPACE CAPSULE

BALLOON

SLED

AUTOMOBILE

PUSHCART

SCOOTER

Wasp–A winged insect with a thin body and a narrow waist. Some wasps sting.

WASPS' NEST

Violet–A sweet-smelling flower that blooms in the spring.

W w

Wagon–A cart with four wheels that is used to pull loads.

COVERED WAGON

Watch–A small clock that can be carried or worn.

POCKET WATCH

WRIST WATCH

Violin–A musical instrument that has four strings and is played with a bow.

BOW

CHIN REST

TUNING PEGS

BRIDGE

Walrus–A large sea animal with two long tusks. It lives in cold places.

TUSKS

Watermelon–A big green fruit that grows on a vine. Its sweet, juicy meat is red.

Whale–A huge sea animal that swims in the ocean but is not a fish. Whales breathe air, and some of them are the biggest animals living today.

SPERM WHALE

NARWHAL

BLUE WHALE

THESE WHALES ARE BIGGER THAN A MAN OR AN ELEPHANT.

KILLER WHALE

Wheel–A round device on a machine or vehicle that turns on its own center.

WAGON WHEEL

SPOKE

HUB CAP

TIRE

AXLE

Wheelbarrow–A vehicle with handles, used to carry loads.

Whistle–A device that makes a shrill sound when air is blown through it.

Wigwam–A kind of tent made by some North American Indians.

TEPEE

WIGWAM

Windmill–A machine for pumping water or grinding grain, powered by the wind.

SAILS

DUTCH WINDMILL

MODERN STEEL WINDMILL

GRINDSTONE

A B C D E F G H I J K L M N O P Q R S T U V W X Y Z

A B C D E F G H I J K L M N O P Q R S T U V W X Y Z

Window–An opening in a building, usually covered with glass, that lets in light and air.

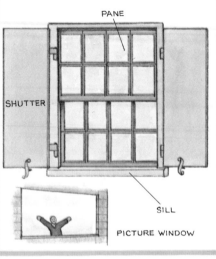

PANE

SHUTTER

SILL

PICTURE WINDOW

Wood–The hard part of a tree or bush found underneath the bark. Many things are made of wood, including paper.

BARK

WOOD

LOG

SAWMILL

TREE

SAWDUST

BOARDS

Witch–A character in books who has magic powers.

Wool–The soft hair of sheep or other animals, used to make yarn or cloth.

SHEEP

YARN

WOOL

Wreath–A ring made of leaves or flowers.

CHRISTMAS WREATH

Wolf–A wild animal in the dog family.

Worm–A small animal with a soft body that has no legs.

EARTHWORM

Wrench–A tool used to turn nuts.

OPEN-END WRENCH

ADJUSTABLE WRENCH

NUT

BOX WRENCH

X x

X-ray–A photograph of the inside of the body, taken with a special camera.

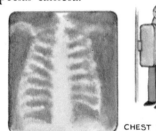

CHEST X-RAY

Xylophone–A musical instrument with bars that make tones when hit with a hammer.

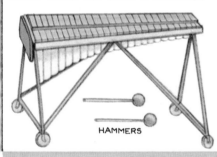

HAMMERS

Y y

Yacht–A boat used for sailing or racing.

Yak–A kind of long-haired ox that lives in Asia.

Yard–A fenced-off piece of ground around a house or other building.

Yardstick–A device for measuring that is three feet, or one yard, long.

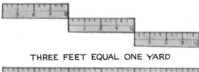

THREE FEET EQUAL ONE YARD

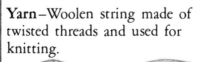

Yarn–Woolen string made of twisted threads and used for knitting.

KNITTING NEEDLES

Yoke–A wooden frame used to fasten two animals together.

YOKE FOR OXEN

Yolk–The yellow center of an egg.

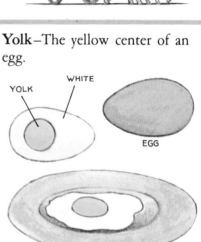

YOLK   WHITE

EGG

Yo-Yo–A spinning toy with a string that is looped around the finger.

A B C D E F G H I J K L M N O P Q R S T U V W X Y Z

A
B
C
D
E
F
G
H
I
J
K
L
M
N
O
P
Q
R
S
T
U
V
W
X
Y
Z

Z z

Zebra–A wild African animal that looks like a small striped horse.

Zeppelin–A huge airship with a rigid frame covered by a thin skin. It is filled with a gas that is lighter than air.

Zero–The number 0, which stands for nothing.

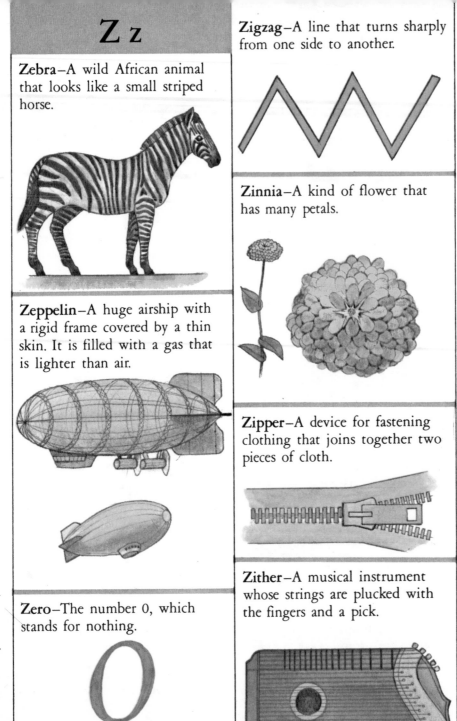

0,1 2 3 4 5 6 7 8 9 10

Zigzag–A line that turns sharply from one side to another.

Zinnia–A kind of flower that has many petals.

Zipper–A device for fastening clothing that joins together two pieces of cloth.

Zither–A musical instrument whose strings are plucked with the fingers and a pick.

Zoo–A place where wild animals are kept so that people can come to look at them.

BIRDHOUSE (AVIARY)

LION HOUSE

BEAR'S DEN

ENTRANCE GATE